IS THIS LOVE.... ?
COLORING BOOK

CRYSTAL
COLORING BOOKS

ISBN-13: 978-1717104939
ISBN-10: 1717104932

HE
WANTS TO
KNOW ABOUT
YOU AND YOUR
LIFE

HE
LOOKS INTO
YOUR
EYES
A LOT

HE
MAKES
NICE
COMPLIMENTS
TO
YOU

HE
CONTACTS
YOU

HE
MAKES YOU FEEL
SAFE

HE
TRUSTS
YOU

HE
RESPECTS
YOUR
OPINION

HE
LETS
YOU SEE YOUR
FRIENDS
AND FAMILY

HE
GETS
JEALOUS

HE
IS ALWAYS
HAPPY
TO SEE
YOU

HIS
VOICE IS
DIFFERENT
WHEN HE TALKS
TO
YOU

HE
CAN'T KEEP
HIS HANDS
OFF
YOU

HE
REMEBERS
LITTLE
DETAILS

HE
STARES
AT YOU
A
LOT

HE
FINDS
REASONS TO
CONTACT
YOU

HE
TAKES YOU OUT
FOR DATES
ALONE

HE
LETS
YOU MEET
HIS
FRIENDS

HE DOES
NOT TALK
ABOUT OTHER
GIRLS WHEN HE
IS WITH
YOU

HE
DOES
THINGS FOR
YOU

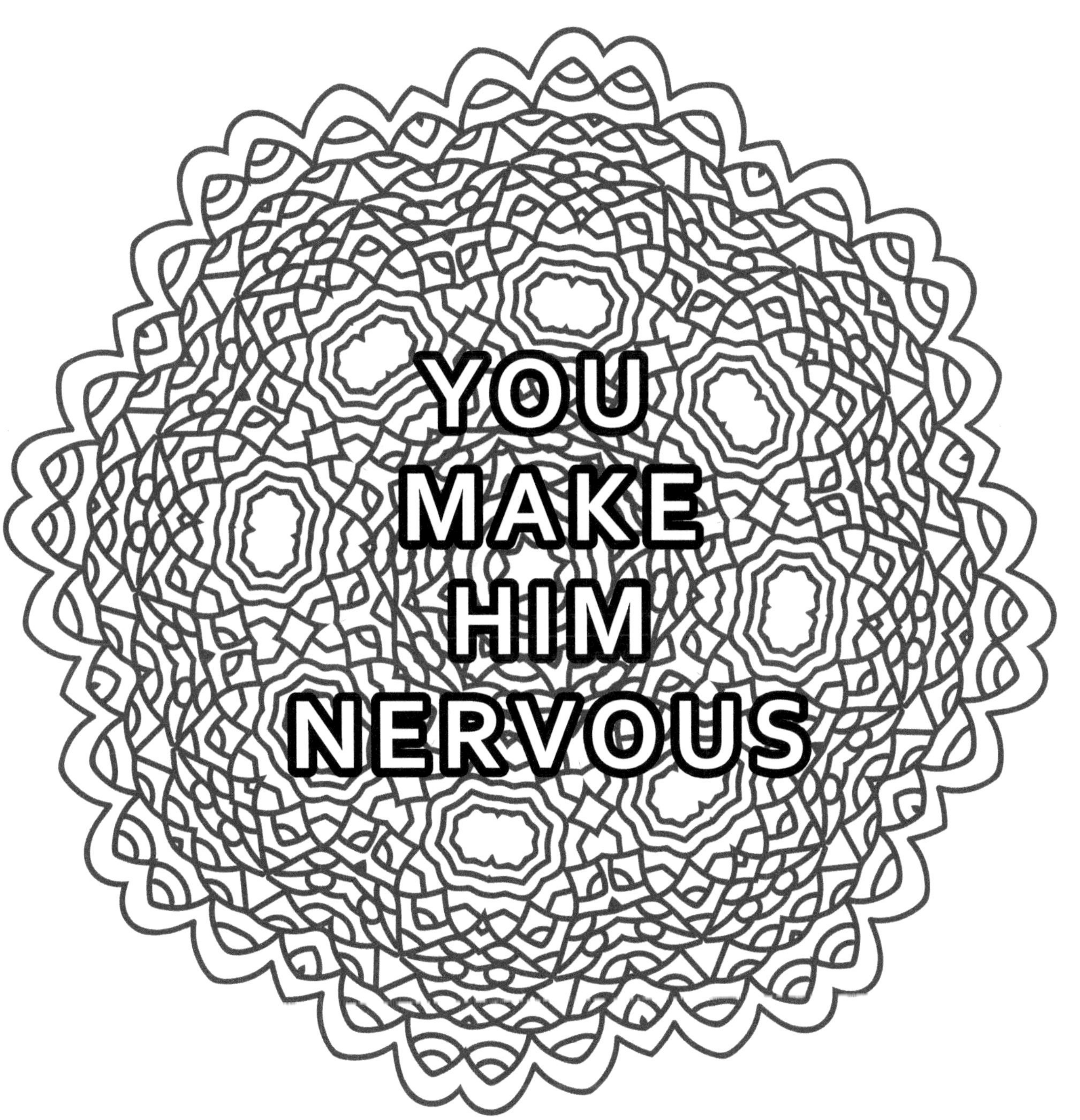

YOU
MAKE
HIM
NERVOUS

COLOR TEST PAGE

www.ingramcontent.com/pod-product-compliance
Lightning Source LLC
Chambersburg PA
CBHW082333270726
48658CB00018B/3258